2003 | Intermediate 2 SQP

[BLANK PAGE]

Intermediate 2

English

Specimen Question Paper for Exams in and after 2003
Close Reading
Critical Essay

2003 Exam
Close Reading
Critical Essay

2004 Exam
Close Reading
Critical Essay

2005 Exam
Close Reading
Critical Essay

2006 Exam
Close Reading
Critical Essay

Leckie × Leckie

First exam published in 2003.

Published by Leckie & Leckie Ltd, 3rd Floor, 4 Queen Street, Edinburgh EH2 1JE

tel: 0131 220 6831 fax: 0131 225 9987 enquiries@leckieandleckie.co.uk www.leckieandleckie.co.uk

ISBN 1-84372-426-X   ISBN-13 978-1-84372-426-1

A CIP Catalogue record for this book is available from the British Library.

Printed in Scotland by Scotprint.

Leckie & Leckie is a division of Granada Learning Limited.

Leckie & Leckie is grateful to the copyright holders, as credited at the back of the book, for permission to use their material. Every effort has been made to trace the copyright holders and to obtain their permission for the use of copyright material. Leckie & Leckie will gladly receive information enabling them to rectify any error or omission in subsequent editions.

[C115/SQP208]

NATIONAL
QUALIFICATIONS

Time: 1 hour

ENGLISH
INTERMEDIATE 2
Close Reading
Specimen Question Paper
(for examinations in and after 2003)

Answer all questions.

30 marks are allocated to this paper.

Read the passage carefully and then answer **all** the questions, **using your own words as far as possible**.

The questions will ask you to show that:

> you understand the main ideas and important details in the passage—in other words, **what** the writer has said (**Understanding—U**);

> you can identify, using appropriate terms, the techniques the writer has used to get across these ideas—in other words, **how** he has said it (**Analysis—A**);

> you can, using appropriate evidence, comment on how effective the writer has been—in other words, **how well** he has said it (**Evaluation—E**).

A code letter (U, A, E) is used alongside each question to identify its purpose for you. The number of marks attached to each question will give some indication of the length of answer required.

SCOTTISH
QUALIFICATIONS
AUTHORITY

©

The passage that follows is adapted from a newspaper article advising scientists how to improve their image.

How to make science loveable

Scientists have been attacked for being too remote. Brian Millar explains how they can win back public support.

"Pay attention," winks Jennifer Aniston in the shampoo ads. "Here comes the science bit." Of course we don't pay attention during the science bit, and Jennifer doesn't expect us to. Few of us paid attention in school during the science bits and fewer still pay attention as adults.

5 Small wonder then that scientists are trusted less than ever before, and are perceived as failing to provide straightforward answers to pressing questions over issues such as BSE and GM foods.

If it's any consolation to scientists, they're not alone. Almost every institution in the UK has seen a significant drop in public confidence over the last decade. The police, the
10 church and the legal system have all taken serious knocks. Confidence in the press has also managed to decline steeply.

Some years ago it was big corporations who had to acknowledge the power that individual consumers had over them. Now it's scientists' turn to feel that the public are turning on them. But they should beware of talking to slick admen about glossy
15 campaigns, and here I speak as a slick adman. Scientists aren't a brand to be packaged and given a superficial makeover. Because of modern politics, we all have highly developed spin detectors. We might tolerate a bit of hype from a shampoo. We won't in a politician or public figure.

It will take more than a new logo on a letterhead and some nice TV spots to change the
20 public's perception of scientists. And the change has to come from scientists themselves.

Luckily, scientists are naturally great communicators—with each other. The sharing of information is culturally ingrained into scientists as with no other community.

They just don't get out enough—or rather, they're not allowed out. Science is hierarchical in a way that few other organisations are anymore. The voices that we hear
25 tend to be either senior academics or PR hacks from large corporations.

There's little or no opportunity for the public to come into contact with the workers at the coal face, the people who might give us the answers we're looking for and not toe the party line. Where do you think you'd get a more satisfactory picture of the safety of Sellafield? The visitor's centre? Or the pub down the road where the boffins knock off
30 for a swifty after work? Exactly.

Now pay attention: here comes the marketing bit. Today, markets are conversations. A revolution is happening in the communications industry: ad copywriters like me are standing back and watching as real people talk to real people. The scandal! Check out any website on books. Most of the reviews there are written by the readers. Last time I
35 looked, one of the Harry Potter novels had more than 2,000 reader comments, and comments on the comments. Every one of them was more honest and informative than the blurb on the back cover.

In my experience, conversations with scientists are always interesting, especially after a few beers. They have the same concerns as the rest of us: they worry about the food
40 their kids eat or whether mobile phones are toasting their brains.

But because they paid attention during the science bit, they are better equipped to answer those questions than the rest of us who chose the gentler path of humanities subjects, with their clean classrooms and chairs with proper lumbar support (what is it with scientists and lab stools?).

45 And when they're tackling those questions in a pub, boffins leave the science bit alone because otherwise they see our eyes glaze over. They speak to our concerns as individuals. They generalise. They speculate. They are not rigorous in their explanations. They become unscientific—like the rest of us.

It's that insight that we need when we are wondering what's lurking in a pack of frozen 50 burgers. That's when we need the voice of somebody who's like us, but who can pronounce "spongiform encephalopathy".

So where should this great conversation between science and the rest of us take place? The internet. It is a perfect medium for public conversation. Ironically it was invented by scientists, to help them spread ideas more efficiently. Now the rest of us have caught 55 up and filled their lovely web full of pop group tribute sites.

The internet is no respecter of hierarchy: news postings by a junior scientist or a 10-year-old kid can sit alongside those of a Nobel Prize winner. The pecking order is different: if you make valid points, if you're entertaining or funny, you get attention. Word spreads: she's interesting; this stuff is unbelievably tedious; this site tells you how 60 Jennifer gets her hair like that.

Of course thousands of conversations with scientists will offer up a much more complex range of views for us to digest, from the rational to the downright eccentric. But we make daily judgements about who we trust and who we don't as part of everyday life. We can take one more in our stride.

65 Do Nobel Prize winners and busy post-doctorate researchers really have the time to hang out on web discussion pages, answering questions from teenagers and loony conspiracy theorists? Bill Gates does. How does this start? Not with formal bodies. The last thing we need is a lovely pristine chat room at the Royal Institution. It needs to come from the 25-year-old who sets him/herself up as thenakedchemist.com (still 70 available), and hundreds and thousands of others. Starting conversations online is easy. Asking and answering questions is easy. If you were bright enough to get a chemistry degree, you can build yourself a website right now and start changing the world. It's not rocket science.

Adapted from an article in *The Telegraph*

Marks *Code*

1. Read the first paragraph (lines 1–4).

   Having considered what the rest of the paragraph says, why do you think Jennifer Aniston winks as she tells us to "pay attention"?   1   U

2. How does the inclusion of the expression "perceived as" (line 5) change the meaning of the sentence in which it appears?   2   A

3. What does the writer mean by an "institution" (line 8), and how does the rest of the paragraph (lines 8–11) help you to understand what he means?   2   A

4. Read lines 12–18.

   (*a*) Giving examples which support your answer, explain how the writer's choice of words underlines his distrust of what he calls "admen".   2   A

   (*b*) **In your own words**, explain what "modern politics" has helped us to develop.   2   U

5. **In your own words**, according to lines 19–25,

   (*a*) what fact about scientists should help them to improve their image?   2   U

   (*b*) what fact about scientists might make it difficult for them to improve their image?   2   U

6. Read lines 31–37.

   (*a*) In the first sentence of this paragraph, the writer echoes the opening of the passage. Why do you think he does this?   1   A

   (*b*) "The scandal!" (line 33)

   What effect does the writer seem to be aiming for in this sentence? What techniques does he use to try to achieve it?   3   A

   (*c*) **In your own words**, what exactly does the writer describe as a "scandal"?   2   U

7. (*a*) Which of the following possibilities is true according to lines 41–44?

   The writer believes that studying science is

   A   more important
   B   more dangerous
   C   more difficult
   D   more profitable

   than studying the humanities subjects.   1   U

   (*b*) How does the writer make this clear?   2   A

8. How does **the structure** of the paragraph in lines 45–48 add to its impact?   2   A

9. (*a*) What is ironic about suggesting the internet as a means for scientists to communicate with ordinary people?   2   U

   (*b*) The writer argues that the internet is the best means for scientists to communicate with ordinary people.

   Referring closely to what he says in the final three paragraphs, clearly explain the arguments that you find most convincing.   4   E

[END OF SPECIMEN QUESTION PAPER]

Total   (30)

[C115/SQP208]

NATIONAL
QUALIFICATIONS

Time: 1 hour 30 minutes

ENGLISH
INTERMEDIATE 2
Critical Essay
Specimen Question Paper
(for examinations in and after 2003)

Answer **two** questions.

Each question must be taken from a different section.

Each question is worth 25 marks.

SCOTTISH
QUALIFICATIONS
AUTHORITY

Answer TWO questions from this paper.

Each question must be chosen from a different Section (A–E). You are not allowed to choose two questions from the same Section.

In all Sections you may use Scottish texts.

Write the number of each question in the margin of your answer booklet and begin each essay on a fresh page. You should spend about 45 minutes on each essay.

The following will be assessed:

- **the relevance of your essays to the questions you have chosen**
- **the quality of your writing**
- **the technical accuracy of your writing.**

Each answer is worth up to 25 marks. The total for this paper is 50 marks.

SECTION A—DRAMA

1. Choose a scene from a play in which a character makes an important decision.

   Say what causes him or her to make the decision and go on to show how the decision affects his or her actions in the rest of the play.

   In your answer you must refer to the text and to at least **two** of: key scene, characterisation, structure, or any other appropriate feature.

2. Choose a play in which one of the characters suffers a breakdown in a relationship with another character.

   Show what the relationship was and go on to explain what makes it break down.

   In your answer you must refer to the text and to at least **two** of: characterisation, key scene(s), climax, or any other appropriate feature.

3. Choose a play in which one of the main concerns is injustice or cruelty or exploitation or betrayal.

   State the main concern and go on to show how the playwright deals with this concern in such a way as to involve your sympathies.

   In your answer you must refer to the text and to at least **two** of: theme, characterisation, key scene(s), or any other appropriate feature.

SECTION B—PROSE

4. Choose one or more prose works (novel, short story(ies), essay(s), journalism) which deal(s) with family or community life.

   Show how differing points of view in the family or community are developed in the work(s) you have chosen, and how they have influenced your thinking.

   In your answer you must refer to the text and to at least **two** of: theme, structure, conflict, or any other appropriate feature.

5. Choose a novel or a short story in which there is an obvious climax or turning point.

   Show how the writer leads up to this turning point or climax, and say what its significance is for the rest of the story.

   In your answer you must refer to the text and to at least **two** of: structure, plot, key incident(s), or any other appropriate feature.

6. Choose a prose work of fiction or non-fiction which creates a sense of time and place.

   Show how the sense of time and place is created and evaluate its importance in your appreciation of the main concerns of the prose work.

   In your answer you must refer to the text, and to at least **two** of: setting, language, theme, or any other appropriate feature.

SECTION C—POETRY

7. Choose a poem which deals with a happy experience.

   Briefly describe the experience and show how the poet has communicated the feelings of happiness by the use of various poetic techniques.

   In your answer you must refer to the text and to at least **two** of: word choice, tone, imagery, structure, or any other appropriate feature.

8. Choose a poem which increased your understanding of any aspect of life in the modern world.

   State what aspect of life in the modern world the poem illustrates and go on to show how the poem, both by its content and by its style, increased your understanding.

   In your answer you must refer to the text and to at least **two** of: ideas, theme, imagery, word choice, or any other appropriate feature.

9. Choose a poem which deals with a particular time of year.

   Show how the poet, by her or his choice of content and skilful use of techniques, helps you to appreciate the positive or negative aspects of the time of year described.

   In your answer you must refer to the text and to at least **two** of: word choice, imagery, tone, ideas, or any other appropriate feature.

SECTION D—MASS MEDIA

10. Choose a film which has an important sequence involving thrilling action such as a chase, a fight, an ambush, or a supernatural event.

Briefly say why the sequence is important, and show how the sequence is made exciting for the audience.

In your answer you must refer to the text and to at least **two** of: use of camera, mise-en-scène, editing, music, or any other appropriate feature.

11. Choose a TV drama, series or serial which has a political, social, or religious theme.

Show how the portrayal of this theme is enhanced by the characters and setting of the drama, series or serial.

In your answer you must refer to the text and to at least **two** of: content, characterisation, mise-en-scène, or any other appropriate feature.

12. Choose a TV series or serial which depends to some extent for its success on humour.

To what extent do you feel the series or serial to be successful because of its humour of situation, or character(s), or both?

In your answer you must refer to the text and to at least **two** of: setting, characterisation, editing, plotting, or any other appropriate feature.

SECTION E—LANGUAGE

13. Choose an aspect of spoken language which you have identified in one age group or locality.

Outline how you gathered your evidence and which aspects of spoken language you focused on. Go on to show the main characteristics of the language you identified, and assess the advantages and disadvantages of these characteristics for communication.

You must refer to specific examples of speech, and to at least **two** features such as: register, accent, dialect, vocabulary, or any other appropriate feature.

14. Choose aspects of language which are commonly used to persuade the reader to think or act favourably towards a particular organisation or group of people.

Show how in the course of your investigation you gained an awareness of the effectiveness of the techniques used to influence you.

You must refer to specific examples and to at least **two** features such as: register, tone, or any other appropriate feature.

15. Choose an aspect of communication (TV, radio, internet, etc) which has made an impact on language within the last twenty years. Explain, with reference to examples you have studied, how you think language has changed and whether you think it has affected the accuracy of communication.

You must refer to specific examples and to at least **two** features such as: register, vocabulary, codes, abbreviation, or any other appropriate feature.

[END OF SPECIMEN QUESTION PAPER]

2003 | Intermediate 2

[BLANK PAGE]

X115/201

NATIONAL
QUALIFICATIONS
2003

FRIDAY, 16 MAY
1.00 PM – 2.00 PM

ENGLISH
INTERMEDIATE 2
Close Reading

Answer all questions.

30 marks are allocated to this paper.

Read the passage carefully and then answer **all** the questions, **using your own words as far as possible**.

The questions will ask you to show that:

> you understand the main ideas and important details in the passage—in other words, **what** the writer has said (**Understanding—U**);

> you can identify, using appropriate terms, the techniques the writer has used to get across these ideas—in other words, **how** he has said it (**Analysis—A**);

> you can, using appropriate evidence, comment on how effective the writer has been—in other words, **how well** he has said it (**Evaluation—E**).

A code letter (U, A, E) is used alongside each question to identify its purpose for you. The number of marks attached to each question will give some indication of the length of answer required.

SCOTTISH
QUALIFICATIONS
AUTHORITY

©

The passage that follows is an excerpt from the fifth chapter of a travel book in which Jonathan Raban describes his fascination with boats.

In 1979 I wandered down the Mississippi in a 16-foot open boat with an outboard motor. There was no element of stunt in the trip; it was the only possible way of encountering a great river at close quarters. I didn't camp out on sandbars, or pretend to be Huckleberry Finn; I stayed in motels, ate in restaurants and drank too much and too
5 long in riverside bars.

Simple possession of a boat turned out to be a ticket of entry to the society of the river. Lock keepers, ferrymen, towboat captains, fishermen, duck hunters treated me as an insider. Within a month of setting off, I could gossip comfortably about chutes, sloughs, sawyers, silting-up bends, wingdams and drownings, adding my own bit to the lore. By
10 the time I was halfway down, and into the beginning of the Mississippi's reaches, I was an accredited river man. Though the oddity of my accent in those parts sometimes marked me out, I never felt less of a tourist, or more easily able to drift into the lives of strangers. We had the river in common, and it was a powerful bond.

When I dumped the unlovely aluminium boat in New Orleans at the end of the trip, I
15 thought I was through with boats in general. I'd spent too much time being afraid, expecting imminent capsize (at the time, I didn't know how safe I really was; the dangers were mostly illusory ones, but none the less powerful for that). The journey had been a good deal more interesting than I'd meant it to be, and I thought I'd better find some way of travelling that didn't keep one's concentration screwed to breaking point.

20 Back in England, I felt quite unexpectedly bereft. After a long night of confused passage making, dodging tows, skidding on boils and racing through chutes, I'd wake up in the morning and remember with a pang, that I'd lost the river and the boat. There was only one way to stop the dreams coming, and I bought a scuffed 15-foot launch which I kept moored on the Thames at Hammersmith. I took it to Lechlade at one end of the river
25 and Tilbury at the other in a succession of soft, suburban outings.

Boat begat boat. My Mississippi book sold well in the United States, and I was able to buy a seagoing ketch and have it refitted for a voyage round the British Isles. The money was meant to be a temporary investment: when I reached Cornwall again the next autumn, the boat would be sold, leaving me out of pocket, since boats, unlike
30 houses, only go down in value.

As for its larger value—I've found a way of keeping on the move that works, or seems to. Accommodation sufficient to contain an ordinary daily working life. A suitable speed at which to meet the world. Just enough danger to keep one's wits sharp. A vehicle dependent on the random chances and decisions of the weather.

35 It travels at a Victorian pace. Under way, with a friendly tide and wind behind it, it will manage seven to eight knots over the ground—say nine m.p.h. at most. At this speed, you can get to know each wave on intimate terms, and if land is in sight you can study it—you have to study it—as closely as a book. Searching for marks, taking bearings, you get to know a coast in the purposeful way of someone whose living literally depends on
40 his comprehension of his own exact place in the landscape.

But it is the wind—the endless shifting gradients of atmospheric pressure—that makes travelling in a small boat into an *adventure*, in the sense defined by the dictionary ("That which happens without design; chance, hap, luck"). The wind blows you into places that you'd never meant to visit, and keeps you pinioned there. The wind is a mad
45 travel agent, with a malicious and surrealist turn of wit. You want to go to France—the wind will maroon you for ten days in Dover. You want to go to the Shetland Islands, and the wind will make you spend a week in Bridlington as penance for your vanity. You can't move without the wind's consent, and when you do move, you find yourself suddenly rescheduled, headed for a destination that you hadn't heard of ten minutes ago.
50 Every day the chart and the pilot book produce surprises; and if you have any sense, you always take the wind's advice and go where it listeth, to the obscure village or small town that offers shelter. Sometimes you have to stay out at sea, missing your original destination altogether. More often, you're driven in haste into harbours you'd overlooked, far short of where you'd planned to be that night.

55 Going by sea is a reliably constant adventure. It's a slow and unpredictable business. It requires patience and a curiosity about those unregarded places in the world where you're forever finding yourself stranded. Since its original circuit of the British Isles, *Gosfield Maiden* has taken me to Ireland, France, Belgium, the Netherlands, West Germany, Denmark and Sweden. In every country, the wind has taken control of the
60 itinerary, landing the boat up, for days on end, in ports that I had no idea I was destined to visit.

From Girvan in Scotland to Hogänäs in Sweden, they were chosen by the weather, these windfall-landfalls. It is true about any port in a storm: as you round the inner breakwater after a few hours out in a rough sea, the dingiest town seems a wonderful
65 place to be. I've come humiliatingly close to kissing the stones of Grimsby fish dock, I was so glad to be there. The worse the weather, the more you love the town—which is useful, since you'll probably have time to learn the name of every single street before the wind will allow you to leave it.

Adapted from *For Love and Money* by Jonathan Raban

QUESTIONS

Marks Code

1. (a) Explain clearly why the writer "wandered down the Mississippi" in his boat. 2 U

   (b) Explain fully how the evidence the writer provides shows that there was "no element of stunt" in the trip. 2 U

2. (a) What **two** reasons does the writer give for feeling that he had become "an accredited river man" (line 11)? 2 U

   (b) What word in the second paragraph (lines 6–13) suggests that the "society of the river" (line 6) has its own history and tradition? 1 A

3. Quote **two** expressions from the first two paragraphs (lines 1–13) which convey the notion of a leisurely journey and experience. 2 A

4. (a) In your own words, describe the writer's reasons for thinking he was "through with boats" (line 15). 2 U

   (b) Quote **two** expressions from lines 20–25 which suggest that the writer nevertheless missed both the boat and the river. 2 A

5. What is the effect of the writer's use of **alliteration** in ". . . a succession of soft, suburban outings." (line 25)? 1 A

6. "I've found a way of keeping on the move that works . . ." (line 31)

   (a) Explain in some detail any **two** of the writer's reasons for believing this. 4 U

   (b) Comment on the sentence structure used in presenting these reasons. 2 A

7. The purpose of lines 41–54 is to illustrate how **the wind** makes travelling in a small boat an adventure.

   Giving an example to support your answer, explain how the writer has used either sentence structure **or** imagery to do this. 2 A

8. ". . . the wind has taken control of the itinerary . . ." (lines 59–60)

   Quote **two** other expressions the writer uses in lines 55–61 to convey this idea. 2 A

9. "It is true about any port in a storm:" (line 63)

   How effective do you find the final paragraph in elaborating on this idea?

   You may wish to consider any **one** feature such as structure, word choice or illustration. 2 E

10. The writer's main purpose in this extract is to convey his fascination with travelling by boat.

    Identify **two** features of style the writer uses and comment on how well you believe he has achieved his purpose. 4 E

Total (30)

[END OF QUESTION PAPER]

X115/202

NATIONAL
QUALIFICATIONS
2003

FRIDAY, 16 MAY
2.20 PM – 3.50 PM

ENGLISH
INTERMEDIATE 2
Critical Essay

Answer **two** questions.

Each question must be taken from a different section.

Each question is worth 25 marks.

SAB X115/202 6/25870

Answer TWO questions from this paper.

Each question must be chosen from a different Section (A–E). You are not allowed to choose two questions from the same Section.

In all Sections you may use Scottish texts.

Write the number of each question in the margin of your answer booklet and begin each essay on a fresh page. You should spend about 45 minutes on each essay.

The following will be assessed:

- **the relevance of your essays to the questions you have chosen**

- **the quality of your writing**

- **the technical accuracy of your writing.**

Each answer is worth up to 25 marks. The total for this paper is 50 marks.

SECTION A—DRAMA

1. Choose a play which has an important scene at a turning point in the play.

   Give a brief account of the scene and go on to show why it is important in the play as a whole.

   In your answer you must refer to the text and to at least **two** of: key scene, structure, characterisation, conflict, or any other appropriate feature.

2. Choose a play which explores relationships within a family, or between two members of a family.

   Describe any such relationship(s) and go on to show how they affect the events of the play.

   In your answer you must refer to the text and to at least **two** of: characterisation, plot, theme, conflict, or any other appropriate feature.

3. Choose a play which deals with an issue of importance to society today.

   State what the issue is and go on to show how, through the plot and characters, the play increased your understanding of this issue.

   In your answer you must refer to the text and to at least **two** of: theme, plot, characterisation, dialogue, or any other appropriate feature.

SECTION B—PROSE

4. Choose a novel or short story where one of the main characters is female.

   Show how the character's contribution to the content and outcome is important in the story as a whole.

   In your answer you must refer to the text and to at least **two** of: characterisation, theme, structure, plot, or any other appropriate feature.

5. Choose **one** or **more than one** work of fiction **or** non-fiction which deals with a serious aspect of life.

   State what this serious aspect is and go on to show how your understanding of it was deepened by your reading of the work(s).

   In your answer you must refer to the text and to at least **two** of: theme, conflict, characterisation, setting, or any other appropriate feature.

6. Choose a novel or short story which has an incident or moment of great tension.

   Describe briefly what happens at this point in the story and go on to show how it is important for the outcome of the story as a whole.

   In your answer you must refer to the text and to at least **two** of: structure, key scene, characterisation, climax, or any other appropriate feature.

SECTION C—POETRY

7. Choose a poem in which a particular place is described, either in the town or in the country.

   Briefly state what the poem is about and then go on to show how the techniques highlight particular aspects of the place, making it seem real to you.

   In your answer you must refer to the text and to at least **two** of: imagery, word choice, structure, tone, or any other appropriate feature.

8. Choose a poem which creates an atmosphere of despair about human existence.

   Show how the poet, by his use of ideas and techniques, leaves you with a pessimistic feeling about life.

   In your answer you must refer to the text and to at least **two** of: mood, word choice, tone, imagery, or any other appropriate feature.

9. Choose a poem in which you find the ending particularly interesting or surprising or satisfying.

   By considering the whole poem say why you think the ending is effective.

   In your answer you must refer to the text and to at least **two** of: structure, ideas, imagery, word choice, or any other appropriate feature.

[Turn over

SECTION D—MASS MEDIA

10. Choose an important scene from a film in which an atmosphere of mystery, or horror, or suspense is created.

    Briefly state what happens in the scene and why it is important to the film as a whole. Go on to show what techniques are used to create the atmosphere of mystery or horror or suspense.

    In your answer you must refer to the text and to at least **two** of: editing, use of camera, characterisation, soundtrack, or any other appropriate feature.

11. Choose a TV drama, series or serial which creates a picture of a community.

    Show how this picture is created and is made realistic for you.

    In your answer you must refer to the text and at least **two** of: sets, characterisation, theme, editing, or any other appropriate feature.

12. Choose a film in which the closing sequence makes use of a variety of film techniques to make its dramatic impact.

    Briefly state what happens in the closing sequence and show how the techniques used make the ending dramatic.

    In your answer you must refer to the text and to at least **two** of: editing, music, use of camera, soundtrack, or any other appropriate feature.

SECTION E—LANGUAGE

13. Consider language which is designed to persuade the reader of the benefits of a product or the rights of a cause.

    Show how in the course of your investigation you gained an awareness of the emotive nature of the language you were dealing with and evaluated its effectiveness.

    You must refer to specific examples, and to concepts such as register, tone, intonation or any other appropriate feature.

14. Consider aspects of spoken language which you have identified in **one** or **more than one** group of people.

    Outline how you gathered your evidence. Go on to show the main similarities and/or differences you identified within the group or between groups, and what conclusions you drew from your findings.

    You must refer to specific examples of speech, and to language concepts such as register, accent, dialect, vocabulary or any other appropriate feature.

15. Consider the language specific to a group which has a common leisure or vocational interest.

    Show to what extent technical terminology used by the group is useful in describing concepts accurately.

    You must refer to specific examples, and to concepts such as technical terminology, jargon, abbreviation or any other appropriate feature.

[END OF QUESTION PAPER]

2004 | Intermediate 2

[BLANK PAGE]

X115/201

NATIONAL
QUALIFICATIONS
2004

FRIDAY, 14 MAY
1.00 PM – 2.00 PM

ENGLISH
INTERMEDIATE 2
Close Reading

Answer all questions.

30 marks are allocated to this paper.

Read the passage carefully and then answer **all** the questions, **using your own words as far as possible**.

The questions will ask you to show that:

> you understand the main ideas and important details in the passage—in other words, **what** the writer has said (**Understanding—U**);

> you can identify, using appropriate terms, the techniques the writer has used to get across these ideas—in other words, **how** he has said it (**Analysis—A**);

> you can, using appropriate evidence, comment on how effective the writer has been—in other words, **how well** he has said it (**Evaluation—E**).

A code letter (U, A, E) is used alongside each question to identify its purpose for you. The number of marks attached to each question will give some indication of the length of answer required.

SCOTTISH
QUALIFICATIONS
AUTHORITY

©

The passage which follows is adapted from an article in the Travel section of a newspaper. In it,
Sean Newsom tells of his experience as a trainee guide in the African bush.

Playing at Guide and Seek

At some point in their lives, everybody has been at this place. Maybe they were waiting
to give a best man's speech with not one good joke in it. Or perhaps it was outside a
school hall before the start of an exam. And I'm pretty sure they all felt the same thing:
as if they had just jumped out of a plane at the start of their first-ever sky dive, and
5 realised they had forgotten their parachute.

In 45 minutes I will lead a walking safari through the African bush – with only five days'
training under my belt. That's right, dear reader: six days ago I knew as much about the
fauna and flora of East Africa as I did about the contents of your fridge. Now I am going
to lead six strangers into a two-mile stretch of savannah and attempt to turn this brown
10 world of dry vegetation and nervous, secretive animals into a colourful and exciting
abundance of biological complexity. And I'm going to attempt to do so without anyone
getting hurt.

Actually, there's very little chance that we are going to meet anything dangerous. This is
the Saadani, not the Serengeti. It's a small game reserve on the coast, north of Dar-es-
15 Salaam, and although there are plenty of animals here – from a kaleidoscope of
kingfishers to a wide range of buck, giraffes and even lions – it's also the site of one of
the oldest settlements in Tanzania. The presence of humans long ago taught the local
carnivore populations who really is the king of the jungle. Just in case one of them
attempts a takeover, however, we're going to be accompanied by an armed warden. Dave
20 will be there too.

That's not what I'm worried about. What really concerns me is the fact that, in order to
make this test a little more "interesting" as he puts it, Dave has decided not to tell his
clients who I am. Bit of a surprise, that. After all, this course is not supposed to be the
real thing. It's more of a taster, at least, that's what I thought. Now, however, I am faced
25 by the prospect of six trusting souls who all think I'm an expert. And I am terrifyingly
short of the information that I need. Don't get me wrong, Dave has done his best to
prepare me for this moment. Working with a specially prepared training manual, he's
introduced me to the vast range of skills that a safari guide needs. We've worked on Jeep
and boat handling, plant and animal identification, tracking, safety, conservation issues
30 and local politics. We've travelled from Dar-es-Salaam to the magnificent and
undeveloped Selous Game Reserve, and then to a beachfront camp in the Saadani. And
all the time, Dave has been talking.

That's the problem, really. Every time he opens his mouth there is something new to
remember. It might be a little titbit of information that is going to liven up a dull
35 moment out in the bush, such as the recent discovery of a whole system of low-
frequency murmurings that elephants use to keep in contact with each other. There's so
much fascinating stuff to learn about this place, and that's before you've got to the tricky
business of remembering what everything is called. One by one, Dave throws names at
me. One by one, I forget them.

40 You can imagine what the walking safari is like. There is a brief moment of triumph at
the start when I manage to get an antlion to perform for us. Antlions are little grubs that
live in the ground and excavate cone-shaped holes in the soil. They're expert hunters
and perfect examples of how murderous the bush is, even when the animals

involved are smaller than your fingernail. They also happen to be a useful way of
45 keeping your clients entertained when there is nothing more glamorous to look at. The
reason why antlions dig their holes is because they want ants to fall into them and
provide them with a meal, and – lo! – just as I'm telling my group this, along comes an
ant and tumbles into the miniature death-pit. He's too big for this particular grub,
however, and after a struggle, he escapes. But he's proved my point perfectly. My clients
50 are excited. So am I.

From then on, however, a more familiar pattern reasserts itself. My warden leads us into
a thicket of whistling thorn acacia that seems to be half a mile thick. I dutifully say my
piece on whistling thorn acacia. After a minute or two, I start to get nervous. After five, I
am beginning to panic.

55 So it's with a huge wash of relief that eventually I spot a medium-sized, brilliantly-
coloured bird, flitting between the trees. "Hey, everyone!" I call. "It's a lilac-backed
roller!" And I take a look through my binoculars. That's when I realise that actually it
doesn't have a lilac-coloured back at all. Its breast is lilac. It's a lilac-breasted roller, one
of the most common birds on the savannah. The kind you never, ever, misidentify. It's as
60 if I've just called a blackbird a robin.

It gets worse. Because when I turn back to see if anybody has noticed, I realise that
they're all looking the other way. The reason? Well, it turns out that we are no more than
50 yards from a small herd of giraffe. Actually, it's 100 yards now. Not only was I the last
to spot them, my shouting has scared them off.

65 By the time we reach the salt flats that mark the end of our route, I am ready to leave
everybody behind and carry on walking into the sea. The sun is beginning to set now,
and there is just enough time to check out the latest animal prints in the sand before we
climb into the waiting Land Rover for the drive home. I sit down next to the driver and
my whole body goes slack with relief.

70 All that lies ahead of me is one last hurdle of embarrassment, when we tell the clients
who I am. Then we'll all go down to the beach, light a big bonfire and drink a lot of beer.
Occasionally, I'll let my head drop back and look up, through the clear Tanzanian air, at
the brilliant night sky. I'll reflect on what an extraordinary week it's been. And I'll ask
the stars to grant me one small request.

75 Can I do that again?

Adapted from an article in *The Sunday Times*

QUESTIONS

Marks Code

1. Explain how the context of the first paragraph helps you to understand what the writer means by ". . . everybody has been at this place." (line 1).

    2 U

2. Look again at lines 6–12.

    (*a*) How does the punctuation help to convey how worried and unprepared the writer feels?

    1 A

    (*b*) How does the writer establish a conversational tone?

    1 A

    (*c*) How does the writer's contrasting word choice in the sentence beginning "Now I am going to lead . . ." (lines 8–9) convey the difficulty of his task?

    2 A

3. Show how the sentence "That's not what I'm worried about." (line 21) is a successful link between paragraphs 3 and 4.

    2 A

4. Look again at lines 21–32.

    What are the writer's two main concerns?

    2 U

5. Comment on the effectiveness of the structure of the final two sentences in lines 38–39.

    2 A

6. In what **two** ways did the writer think the antlion's performance provided him with ". . . a brief moment of triumph . . ." (line 40)?

    2 U

7. "From then on, however, a more familiar pattern reasserts itself." (line 51)

    Why does the writer describe the pattern in this way?

    2 U

8. Which expression from lines 51–54 shows that the writer lacks enthusiasm for this part of his task?

    1 U

9. (*a*) Look again at lines 55–60.

    Identify by example any **two techniques** the writer uses to convey his stupidity, and comment on their effectiveness.

    4 E

    (*b*) Why does the writer feel a "huge wash of relief" when he sees a "brilliantly-coloured bird" (lines 55–56)?

    1 U

10. Explain clearly why the writer feels "It gets worse." (line 61).

    2 U

11. What image does the writer use in the second last paragraph (lines 70–74) to show that he felt the safari had been an ordeal, and how does it do so?

    2 A

12. Explain how the short final paragraph (line 75) achieves its impact.

    2 A

13. In what ways might "Playing at Guide and Seek" be considered a particularly appropriate title for this article?

    2 E

Total (30)

[END OF QUESTION PAPER]

X115/202

NATIONAL
QUALIFICATIONS
2004

FRIDAY, 14 MAY
2.20 PM – 3.50 PM

ENGLISH
INTERMEDIATE 2
Critical Essay

Answer **two** questions.

Each question must be taken from a different section.

Each question is worth 25 marks.

SCOTTISH
QUALIFICATIONS
AUTHORITY

Answer TWO questions from this paper.

Each question must be chosen from a different Section (A–E). You are not allowed to choose two questions from the same Section.

In all Sections you may use Scottish texts.

Write the number of each question in the margin of your answer booklet and begin each essay on a fresh page. You should spend about 45 minutes on each essay.

The following will be assessed:

- **the relevance of your essays to the questions you have chosen**

- **the quality of your writing**

- **the technical accuracy of your writing.**

Each answer is worth up to 25 marks. The total for this paper is 50 marks.

SECTION A—DRAMA

1. Choose a play in which one of the main characters has to overcome difficulties in the course of the action.

   State what the difficulties are and show how the character's strengths allow him or her to overcome them.

   In your answer you must refer to the text and to at least **two** of: characterisation, plot, key scenes, theme, or any other appropriate feature.

2. Choose a play in which there is conflict between two important characters.

   Show how the conflict arises and go on to explain how, by the end of the play, it is or is not resolved.

   In your answer you must refer to the text and to at least **two** of: characterisation, dialogue, key scenes, structure, or any other appropriate feature.

3. Choose a play with a violent theme.

   State what the theme is and show how the characters deal with the issues in such a way as either to overcome the violence or to be destroyed by it.

   In your answer you must refer to the text and to at least **two** of: theme, characterisation, climax, key scenes, or any other appropriate feature.

SECTION B—PROSE

4. Choose a novel or short story which deals with family life.

   Show how the relationships within the family affect the events and outcome of the story.

   In your answer you must refer to the text and to at least **two** of: plot, key scenes, characterisation, or any other appropriate feature.

5. Choose a novel or a short story which has an unexpected ending.

   By looking at the story as a whole explain why the ending is surprising, and explain whether you found it satisfactory or not.

   In your answer you must refer to the text and to at least **two** of: structure, characterisation, plot, climax, or any other appropriate feature.

6. Choose a prose work or group of prose works (fiction or non-fiction) dealing to some extent with a less pleasant side of life.

   Show how this less pleasant side of life is portrayed and made more real for you by the description of the people and/or places and/or events.

   In your answer you must refer to the text, and to at least **two** of: theme, language, structure, setting, or any other appropriate feature.

SECTION C—POETRY

7. Choose a poem which deals with a real or imaginary person or place.

   Show how the person or place is introduced and how the techniques used give a convincing portrayal of that person or place.

   In your answer you must refer to the text and to at least **two** of: characterisation, imagery, word choice, tone, or any other appropriate feature.

8. Choose a poem which takes an optimistic view of life.

   Briefly state what the poem is about and go on to show how the techniques used convey these optimistic feelings.

   In your answer you must refer to the text and to at least **two** of: theme, imagery, word choice, structure, or any other appropriate feature.

9. Choose a poem which tells an exciting or frightening story.

   Briefly state what the story is and go on to show how the techniques used make the poem exciting or frightening.

   In your answer you must refer to the text and to at least **two** of: tone, word choice, imagery, rhythm, or any other appropriate feature.

[Turn over

SECTION D—MASS MEDIA

10. Choose a film or *TV drama which has war as its subject.

Show how the film, by its use of content and techniques, has brought home to you the reality of the terrible nature of war.

In your answer you must refer to the text and to at least **two** of: theme, editing, use of camera, music, or any other appropriate feature.

11. Choose a film or *TV drama which deals with conflict within the family.

Show what conflict within the family is portrayed and show what media techniques are used to make the conflict dramatic.

In your answer you must refer to the text and to at least **two** of: characterisation, editing, use of camera, mise-en-scène, or any other appropriate feature.

12. Choose a film or *TV drama which deals with the subject of "good versus evil".

Briefly explain the struggle and show how your sympathy was engaged on one side or the other.

In your answer you must refer to the text and to at least **two** of: characterisation, editing, mise-en-scène, or any other appropriate feature.

* "TV drama" may be a single play, series or serial.

SECTION E—LANGUAGE

13. Consider examples of language used by at least **two** different newspapers or magazines.

Describe the differences which you have noticed and discuss what you think causes these differences.

You must refer to specific examples, and to at least **two** of: register, typography, point of view, or any other appropriate feature.

14. Consider the spoken language of a particular place, for example a town, a city, an area, a country.

What are some of the main features which are important in making this language a distinctive way of speaking? What are the advantages or disadvantages for people speaking this distinctive language?

You must refer to specific examples, and to at least **two** of: dialect, vocabulary, accent, or any other appropriate feature.

15. Consider language used in campaigns designed to influence people's behaviour in a particular area of their lives, for example to improve their health, to support a charity or other organisation, to buy certain products.

Explain how the language is designed to influence people, and whether you think it succeeds in affecting their behaviour.

You must refer to specific examples and to at least **two** of: tone, emotive vocabulary, slogans, or any other appropriate feature.

[END OF QUESTION PAPER]

[BLANK PAGE]

[BLANK PAGE]

X115/201

NATIONAL QUALIFICATIONS 2005	FRIDAY, 13 MAY 1.00 PM – 2.00 PM	ENGLISH INTERMEDIATE 2 Close Reading

Answer all questions.

30 marks are allocated to this paper.

Read the passage carefully and then answer **all** the questions, **using your own words as far as possible**.

The questions will ask you to show that:

you understand the main ideas and important details in the passage—in other words, **what** the writer has said (**Understanding—U**);

you can identify, using appropriate terms, the techniques the writer has used to get across these ideas—in other words, **how** he has said it (**Analysis—A**);

you can, using appropriate evidence, comment on how effective the writer has been—in other words, **how well** he has said it (**Evaluation—E**).

A code letter (U, A, E) is used alongside each question to identify its purpose for you. The number of marks attached to each question will give some indication of the length of answer required.

SCOTTISH
QUALIFICATIONS
AUTHORITY

©

In this extract from the opening chapter of his book, Ralph Storer reflects upon his need to climb mountains.

Why?

It occurs to all of us at one time or another. Perhaps we are gasping for air on some interminable mountain slope that seems to get steeper at every step without bringing us any closer to the elusive summit. Perhaps we are trembling on some disintegrating rock ledge from where all routes onward seem to involve moves at which Spiderman would
5 baulk. Perhaps we are huddled behind a scrap of cairn on some windswept ridge while the blizzard howls around us. Perhaps we are standing knee-deep in a morass of sodden peat that we were confident would hold our weight. It is in situations like this that it hits us: why am I doing this?

From whence comes this compulsion to climb mountains? My neighbours seem to be
10 able to enjoy lives of quiet contentment without ever having to leave the horizontal plane. Why do I have this compulsion to get to the top of every insignificant bump on the landscape? I ponder this question not in the hope of providing an explanation for my neighbours, still less in the hope of converting them, but out of a need to explain this outlandish behaviour to myself. If I am to climb mountains I would simply like to know
15 why. Why, no matter how breathless, bruised, battered and bedraggled I become while hillwalking, do I return with a grin on my face and a desire to go out and do it again?

The first thought that occurs to me is not *why* but *why not*? Our close relatives the apes enjoy climbing, so why not us? Perhaps the desire to get to the top of things is an ancient animal drive that modern society has suppressed. After all, a society geared to
20 material gain can hardly be expected to support such an unproductive pursuit (the only material gain I've made on the hill is finding a glove that didn't fit). Then again, perhaps the act of climbing is simply too ape-like and unsophisticated for most; it is difficult, for example, to maintain any semblance of dignity while lying spread-eagled on the ground after having tripped over a clump of heather. Ironically, the freedom to
25 adopt such a position and have no-one give disapproving looks is one of the secret joys of hillwalking . . . The Great Outdoors is a giant funhouse where we can cast off adult worries and become carefree kids again. It's no accident that children love climbing.

Yet there must be more to it than a desire to have fun, or else why do I keep going when it ceases to be fun? When I'm cold and tired and out of breath, why do I keep putting
30 one foot in front of the other and, when I've returned to the comfort of my home, why do I recall these times with a glow of satisfaction? Perhaps it has something to do with exercise and fitness — the feelgood feeling that comes from muscles that don't ache when you climb stairs, lungs that don't wheeze when you run for a bus and endorphins that buzz round your head and keep you feeling high even after you have returned to
35 sea-level.

I have heard those whose brains have become as useless as their legs equate hillwalking to banging your head against a brick wall, reasoning that you feel good afterwards simply because you have stopped. Such people, perhaps equating effort with pain in order to justify their own laziness, do not appear to be able to appreciate that effort can be
40 rewarding. Moreover, there are some hillwalkers who seem to find the activity hardly any effort at all. I have a friend who is "naturally" fit, whatever that means. He smokes, drinks and leads a generally debauched life, but stand him at the foot of a hill, let go of him and he will leave even Naismith trailing in his wake.

45 Bill Naismith, the "father" of the Scottish Mountaineering Club, is a hard man to keep up with at the best of times, even though the ground hasn't seen the imprint of his boots for some time now. If you can keep to his pace of three miles per hour plus one thousand feet per half hour (metricated to five kilometres per hour plus one hundred metres per ten minutes), count yourself fit. On British hills that is normally a pace most walkers can only attain in dreams.

50 But why do I exert myself on the hill rather than on an athletics track or a tennis court? And why do I find myself exploring the limits of my fitness? Sometimes, after reaching the first summit, I go on to a second. In my more bewildered moments, with my eyes on the ground and my feet firmly in the clouds, I have even been known to climb two separate mountains on the same day. Now that's serious.

55 Perhaps it has something to do with the challenge. I am sometimes amazed by what I will attempt on the hill, but I am also amazed by what I learn about myself by doing so and perhaps this is why I do it. On the other hand, cycling around city streets is just as risky and physically challenging, so there has to be something still more to it. Perhaps it has something to do with the environment in which hillwalking takes place — outside,
60 away from city streets, in air that has not been breathed by others.

In Victorian times people took to the seaside to escape the dark satanic mills; now it is the countryside that beckons. They say it began in the depressed thirties, when northerners escaped to the Lake District, midlanders to North Wales and lowland Scots to the Highlands. I know the pull, having myself been job-bound in the Big Smoke and
65 desperate to get away. Some citydwellers become so conditioned to city life that they cannot live without the noise and bustle of traffic and a regular intake of carbon monoxide; they may well prove to be a mutant species, an evolutionary dead-end divorced from the mainstream of life. If pushed I will grudgingly admit to an understanding of the excitements of city life, but I also need my Arcadian fix. I need
70 terrain other than concrete, greenery other than lawns, an horizon more distant than the end of the street, weather I cannot shelter from and smells from which I am not insulated. Without these I wither away like a plant without light.

Adapted from *The Joy of Hillwalking* by Ralph Storer

QUESTIONS

Marks Code

1. Look at lines 1–8.

   (*a*) Quote **two** expressions which make hillwalking sound a rather unpleasant and uncomfortable activity.

   2 **A**

   (*b*) Quote the **word** which the writer uses to suggest that sometimes the summit seems beyond reach.

   1 **A**

2. "It occurs to all of us at one time or another." (line 1)

   From your reading of the whole paragraph explain what "It" is.

   1 **A**

3. In lines 9–16, the writer reflects on his need to climb mountains.

   By referring to **one** example of each, show how he demonstrates this need through:

   (*a*) word choice;

   2 **A**

   (*b*) sentence structure.

   2 **A**

4. Read lines 17–27 again.

   In your own words, give the **two** reasons the writer uses to explain people's desire to climb hills. Quote briefly to support each reason.

   4 **U**

5. Explain how the sentence "Yet there must be more to . . . it ceases to be fun?" (lines 28–29) performs a linking function.

   2 **A**

6. Using your own words as far as possible, summarise the **three** reasons the writer gives in lines 31–35 for returning to the hills despite all the obvious discomforts.

   3 **U**

7. Look at lines 36–40.

   What is the writer's attitude towards those who do not appreciate hillwalking? Justify your answer by **two** close references to the text.

   3 **U/A**

8. What is suggested by the comment about Naismith that "the ground hasn't seen the imprint of his boots for some time now"? (lines 45–46)

   1 **U**

9. In lines 55–60, the writer begins two sentences with "Perhaps".

   (*a*) How does this word link with the previous paragraph (lines 50–54)?

   1 **A**

   (*b*) What effect does it have on the tone of this paragraph (lines 55–60)?

   1 **A**

10. Look again at the sentence "In Victorian times people took to the seaside to escape the dark satanic mills; now it is the countryside that beckons." (lines 61–62)

    Identify and give an example of **one** technique the writer uses to achieve the effect of balance or contrast.

    2 **A**

11. In the final paragraph (lines 61–72), the writer describes how it is not new for people to be "desperate to get away". With reference to **one** example explain fully, in your own words, how he illustrates this point.

    2 **U**

12. "Without these I wither away like a plant without light." (line 72)

    Comment on the effectiveness of this sentence as a conclusion to the whole passage.

    3 **E**

[END OF QUESTION PAPER]

Total (30)

X115/202

NATIONAL
QUALIFICATIONS
2005

FRIDAY, 13 MAY
2.20 PM – 3.50 PM

ENGLISH
INTERMEDIATE 2
Critical Essay

Answer **two** questions.

Each question must be taken from a different section.

Each question is worth 25 marks.

Answer TWO questions from this paper.

Each question must be chosen from a different Section (A–E). You are not allowed to choose two questions from the same Section.

In all Sections you may use Scottish texts.

Write the number of each question in the margin of your answer booklet and begin each essay on a fresh page. You should spend about 45 minutes on each essay.

The following will be assessed:

- **the relevance of your essays to the questions you have chosen**

- **the quality of your writing**

- **the technical accuracy of your writing.**

Each answer is worth up to 25 marks. The total for this paper is 50 marks.

SECTION A—DRAMA

1. Choose a play in which **one** of the main characters has to cope with strong feelings such as love, jealousy, ambition, hatred.

   Show how the character deals with these feelings and what effect this has on the outcome of the play.

   In your answer you must refer to the text and at least **two** of: characterisation, theme, structure, or any other appropriate feature.

2. Choose a scene from a play in which a conflict between two characters reaches a climax.

   Explain the origins of the conflict and show how the outcome of the scene influences the rest of the play.

   In your answer you must refer to the text and to at least **two** of: structure, characterisation, plot, or any other appropriate feature.

3. Choose a play which explores relationships within a family or community.

   What strengths and/or weaknesses are apparent in these relationships and what is the overall effect on the family or community?

   In your answer you must refer to the text and to at least **two** of: characterisation, theme, structure, or any other appropriate feature.

SECTION B—PROSE

4. Choose a novel or short story in which a character changes in the course of the story.

   What factors seem to cause the development? What effect does this have on the character and on the outcome of the story?

   In your answer you must refer to the text and to at least **two** of: characterisation, plot, key incident, or any other appropriate feature.

5. Choose a prose work or a group of prose works (fiction or non-fiction) which deals with a topic of interest to you.

   Explain how your interest was aroused and how the treatment of the theme or topic contributed to your enjoyment of the work.

   In your answer you must refer to the text and to at least **two** of: theme, ideas, description, structure, or any other appropriate feature.

6. Choose a novel or short story in which you feel there is an incident of great importance.

   Briefly describe the incident and go on to highlight its importance in the story as a whole.

   In your answer you must refer to the text and to at least **two** of: structure, characterisation, plot, climax, or any other appropriate feature.

SECTION C—POETRY

7. Choose a poem which creates a mood of calm, or reflection, or nostalgia.

   Show how the poet creates this mood by the choice of subject matter and by the use of particular poetic techniques.

   In your answer you must refer to the text and to at least **two** of: content, word choice, tone, sound, or any other appropriate feature.

8. Choose a poem which describes a positive experience.

   Describe what happens in the poem, and show how the poet, by the use of poetic techniques, has enhanced your appreciation of the positive aspects of the poem.

   In your answer you must refer to the text and to at least **two** of: word choice, tone, imagery, sound, or any other appropriate feature.

9. Choose a poem which deepens your understanding of human nature.

   State what particular aspect of human nature is explored and show how the poet's choice of content and use of poetic techniques deepens your understanding.

   In your answer you must refer to the text and to at least **two** of: content, word choice, theme, imagery, or any other appropriate feature.

[Turn over

SECTION D—MASS MEDIA

10. Choose a film in which there is a sequence of great importance to the development of character and/or plot.

    Show how elements of character and/or plot are developed in this sequence to create impact.

    In your answer you must refer to the text and to at least **two** of: use of camera, characterisation, editing, sound effects, or any other appropriate feature.

11. Choose a film or TV drama* in which the portrayal of the setting is very important to the success of the film or TV drama.

    Show how the setting is used to increase your appreciation of character and theme in the film or TV drama.

    In your answer you must refer to the text and to at least **two** of: mise-en-scène, use of camera, editing, or any other appropriate feature.

12. Choose a film or TV drama* which seems to reflect contemporary society.

    How successful do you feel the film or TV drama is in convincing the audience that it is giving a true reflection of society today?

    In your answer you must refer to the text and to at least **two** of: theme, setting, dialogue, characterisation, or any other appropriate feature.

    * "TV drama" may be a single play, series or serial.

SECTION E—LANGUAGE

13. Consider your own use of spoken language in different situations.

    Give examples of what the different situations are and go on to discuss how these different situations affect your use of spoken language.

    In your answer you must refer to specific examples and to at least **two** concepts such as context, register, dialect, accent, or any other appropriate feature.

14. Consider the language of advertisements.

    By looking closely at the language of TWO advertisements, state which one you think is more effective in persuading you to buy the product.

    In your answer you must refer to specific examples and to at least **two** concepts such as tone, typography, emotive vocabulary, or any other appropriate feature.

15. Consider aspects of vocabulary connected with the use of the Internet.

    Examine some of the words associated with the use of the Internet and consider how helpful this language is for the general user.

    In your answer you must refer to specific examples and to at least **two** concepts such as jargon, abbreviations, imagery, or any other appropriate feature.

[END OF QUESTION PAPER]

2006 | Intermediate 2

X115/201

NATIONAL
QUALIFICATIONS
2006

FRIDAY, 12 MAY
1.00 PM – 2.00 PM

ENGLISH
INTERMEDIATE 2
Close Reading

Answer all questions.

30 marks are allocated to this paper.

Read the passage carefully and then answer **all** the questions, **using your own words as far as possible**.

The questions will ask you to show that:

> you understand the main ideas and important details in the passage—in other words, **what** the writer has said (**Understanding—U**);

> you can identify, using appropriate terms, the techniques the writer has used to get across these ideas—in other words, **how** he has said it (**Analysis—A**);

> you can, using appropriate evidence, comment on how effective the writer has been—in other words, **how well** he has said it (**Evaluation—E**).

A code letter (U, A, E) is used alongside each question to identify its purpose for you. The number of marks attached to each question will give some indication of the length of answer required.

SCOTTISH
QUALIFICATIONS
AUTHORITY

©

Women and chocolate: Simply made for each other

Women and chocolate are a dream team and advertisers have cleverly ensured they stay that way.

You can bet that when the first Aztec tentatively crushed a cacao bean, right behind him was an ad executive excitedly branding the muddy brown discovery "the food of the gods". Or if there wasn't, there certainly should have been—because chocolate hasn't looked back since. Mars' new "Mars Delight" is just the latest attempt to beguile us into
5 seeing that a mixture of fat, sugar and a type of caffeine is an essential part of our life.

The secret of chocolate's particular appeal lies in the cocoa butter—it melts just below body temperature—which gives it that delicious dissolve-in-the-mouth feeling. Add to that the sudden charge of energy you get from the sugar, the kick of the caffeine and another chemical, which acts as a mood enhancer—and you can understand why the
10 Aztecs originally decreed that only nobles, priests and warriors were allowed to eat it. Then it was seen as the cure for all ills. And it's true—as the confectionery industry is keen to point out—that cocoa beans contain flavonoids which help high blood pressure. And chocolate doesn't have the teeth-rotting qualities of other sweets.

But that's more than counterbalanced by the fact that it's still crammed full of fats and
15 sugar. "We are looking at 9 to 10 calories per gram," says Professor Tom Sanders, the head of nutritional sciences at King's College, London. "And while people admit to eating 18 grams of chocolate a day, the manufacturers think it's nearer 35 grams, about the size of a Crunchie bar. What's also worrying is the trend to "super-size" that we also see in the fast food industry that means that people end up consuming more. Of
20 particular concern is that chocolate bars contain vegetable fats—also known as trans fatty acids (TFAs)—which have been linked to coronary heart disease." Last summer both Nestlé and Cadbury said they were thinking of removing TFAs from their products.

"The Government recommends that less than 2 per cent of dietary energy comes from trans fats," says Hannah Theobald, nutrition scientist at the British Nutrition
25 Foundation. "It is good news that the food industry is looking at ways to reduce them in food products."

Ironically, these concerns are far removed from chocolate's beginnings—when, being made by teetotal Quakers, it was originally promoted here as a healthy alternative to alcohol. One of the first recorded advertisements was a couple of lines in the
30 Birmingham Gazette of March 1, 1824, placed by a John Cadbury. It read: "John Cadbury is desirous of introducing to particular notice 'Cocoa Nibs' prepared by himself, an article affording a most nutritious beverage for breakfast".

The nutritious link was one that early chocolate marketing followed. During the Second World War, manufacturers Caley's urged that female air raid wardens should be bought
35 a box of their Fortune chocolates not just because they'd enjoy them but because it would supply the "extra nutrition to keep them going". Early Mars advertising informed women that there was a "whole meal" in a bar to "nourish, energise and sustain".

"Women are the key to chocolate advertising," says Rita Clifton, the chair of the leading
40 branding agency Interbrand. "They are not only important consumers in their own right but they also act as gatekeepers to the rest of the family. So it's important to get the approach right." So as women's role in society changed so did the chocolate bars and advertising. Out went the stoic "meal on the run" idea, in came the post-Sixties "Me" sense of indulgence—running through fields or sitting in a bath eating a flaky chocolate
45 bar. "One of the most 'indulgent' adverts is the Flake one," Clifton says. "This is the

ultimate example of taking time out for yourself. OK, I could never quite see the point of eating a Flake in the bath—not very practical, but then fantasies aren't meant to be."

But experts say that in recent years the style has changed again. The Milk Tray man was kicked out in favour of the slogan "love with a lighter touch". The fashion,
50 according to Yusuf Chuku, a communications analyst at Naked Communications, is very much towards a lighter, more sophisticated approach. "Because of concerns about advertising to children, I think there's been even more of a move towards targeting women," Chuku says. "With health advice constantly changing, I think advertising is now less about the guilty secret idea, but saying it's OK to eat some chocolate as long as
55 you balance it with other things."

That's reflected in the different types of chocolate being developed—low calorie bars like Flyte, "lighter" bars than the monolithic-looking Mars or Snickers, or developments like Kit Kat Kubes, which can be shared among friends. It also explains the increased demand for organic or more exotic chocolates: if women are going to indulge, they want
60 to make sure it is with a high quality brand. Chuku says that in a competitive market worth £5 billion a year in the UK, no manufacturer can afford to miss which way the wind is blowing: "I think the next trend will be turning back to comforting chocolates you remember from your childhood. Watch out for the Wagon Wheel."

Glenda Cooper, in *The Times Body and Soul* (slightly adapted)

QUESTIONS   *Marks Code*

1. Explain what is meant by the idea that chocolate "hasn't looked back" (lines 3–4) since it was discovered.   **1 U/A**

2. Identify and briefly explain any example of humour from the first paragraph.   **2 A**

3. Explain **in your own words** two of the reasons why chocolate has its "particular appeal". (line 6)   **2 U**

4. Explain why "But that's more than counterbalanced" (line 14) is an appropriate or effective link between the paragraph it begins and the previous one.   **2 A/E**

5. Explain **in your own words** the **two** concerns of Professor Tom Sanders (line 15) about people's chocolate consumption.   **2 U**

6. Why is it "good news" (line 25) that manufacturers are considering reducing the amount of fatty acids in their products?   **1 U**

7. Explain fully why "Ironically" (line 27) is an appropriate choice of word at this point in the passage.   **3 A/E**

8. (*a*) Look at the advertisement placed by John Cadbury (lines 30–32). Comment on the **word choice** or **tone**.   **1 A**

   (*b*) "The nutritious link was one that early chocolate marketing followed." (line 33)

   Write down an expression from the rest of this paragraph, apart from "nutrition" or "nourish", which continues the idea of nourishment.   **1 U**

9. Explain how effective "gatekeepers" (line 41) is as an image or metaphor.   **2 E**

10. (*a*) How does the writer's **word choice** in the sentence beginning "Out went" (line 43) make clear to the reader the changing role of women in society?   **2 U/A**

    (*b*) How does the **structure** of this sentence reinforce this idea of change?   **2 A**

11. Explain fully why the word "fantasies" (line 47) is appropriate to describe the ideas behind the Flake advertisement.   **2 A**

12. Look at the expression "kicked out". (line 49)

    Suggest **two** things this implies about the way people in the advertising industry conduct their business.   **2 U/A**

13. There are "different types of chocolate being developed". (line 56)

    Explain **in your own words two** ways in which these new products would help consumers to think that "it's OK to eat some chocolate". (line 54)   **2 U**

14. "Watch out for the Wagon Wheel." (line 63)

    (*a*) What can you deduce about what the Wagon Wheel was?   **1 U**

    (*b*) Give **two** reasons why this sentence might be an effective advertising slogan.   **2 A/E**

Total (30)

[END OF QUESTION PAPER]

X115/202

NATIONAL
QUALIFICATIONS
2006

FRIDAY, 12 MAY
2.20 PM – 3.50 PM

ENGLISH
INTERMEDIATE 2
Critical Essay

Answer **two** questions.

Each question must be taken from a different section.

Each question is worth 25 marks.

SCOTTISH
QUALIFICATIONS
AUTHORITY
©

Answer TWO questions from this paper.

Each question must be chosen from a different Section (A–E). You are not allowed to choose two questions from the same Section.

In all Sections you may use Scottish texts.

Write the number of each question in the margin of your answer booklet and begin each essay on a fresh page.

You should spend about 45 minutes on each essay.

The following will be assessed:

- **the relevance of your essays to the questions you have chosen**

- **your knowledge and understanding of key elements, central concerns and significant details of the chosen texts**

- **your explanation of ways in which aspects of structure/style/language contribute to the meaning/effect/impact of the chosen texts**

- **your evaluation of the effectiveness of the chosen texts, supported by detailed and relevant evidence**

- **the quality and technical accuracy of your writing.**

Each question is worth 25 marks. The total for this paper is 50 marks.

SECTION A—DRAMA

Answers to questions in this section should refer to the text and to such relevant features as: characterisation, key scene(s), structure, climax, theme, plot, conflict, setting . . .

1. Choose a play in which a character loses the support of her/his friends or family during the course of the play.

   What reasons are there for this loss of support and what effect does this lack of support have on the character's fate in the play?

2. Choose a play which you feel has a memorable opening scene or section.

   Show how the content or atmosphere of the scene or section provides an effective starting point for the development of the characters and the theme of the play.

3. Choose a play in which a character hides the truth from other characters in the play.

   State what the character hides and show how the revealing of the truth affects the outcome of the play.

SECTION B—PROSE

> *Answers to questions in this section should refer to the text and to such relevant features as: characterisation, setting, language, key incident(s), climax/turning point, plot, structure, narrative technique, theme, ideas, description . . .*

4. Choose a novel **or** short story which deals with an important human issue: for example, poverty, war, family conflict, injustice, or any other issue you regard as important.

   State what the issue is and show how the characters cope with the issue in the course of the novel or short story.

5. Choose a novel **or** short story in which the main character makes an important decision.

   Explain why a decision is necessary and go on to show how the decision affects the rest of the novel or short story.

6. Choose a non-fiction text or group of texts which presents you with an interesting place **or** topic.

   Briefly identify the place or topic and go on to show how the writer's presentation made this interesting to you.

SECTION C—POETRY

> *Answers to questions in this section should refer to the text and to such relevant features as: word choice, tone, imagery, structure, content, rhythm, theme, sound, ideas . . .*

7. Choose a poem which deals with birth **or** death **or** love **or** hate **or** jealousy.

   By looking at the content and language of the poem show how your understanding of one of these topics is deepened by your reading of the poem.

8. Choose a poem which deals with nature or the natural world.

   State what aspect of nature is being described and show how the use of poetic techniques deepens your understanding and appreciation of the topic.

9. Choose a poem which arouses strong emotion in you.

   State what it is about the subject of the poem which makes you feel strongly, and go on to show how the poet's use of language reinforces these feelings.

[Turn over

SECTION D—FILM AND TV DRAMA

> *Answers to questions in this section should refer to the text and to such relevant features as: use of camera, key sequence, characterisation, mise-en-scène, editing, setting, music/sound effects, plot, dialogue . . .*

10. Choose a film which has a child or young person as its main character.

    Show how the character is introduced in the film in such a way that you realise he/she is important.

11. Choose a film or TV drama* which raises awareness of an important social issue.

    Identify the issue and show how its importance is brought home to you through the characters who convey these ideas to you.

12. Choose a film or TV drama* which involves conflict between two groups of people.

    Explain the reasons for the conflict and show how the portrayal of the conflict is highlighted by the use of media techniques.

    * "TV drama" includes a single play, a series or a serial.

SECTION E—LANGUAGE

> *Answers to questions in this section should refer to the text and to such relevant features as: register, accent, dialect, slang, jargon, vocabulary, tone, abbreviation . . .*

13. Consider the use of persuasive language in the field of politics, **or** charitable campaigns, **or** commercial advertising.

    Show how the language tries to persuade you and discuss how successful it is in its aim.

14. Consider the differences in spoken language between two groups—for example, the inhabitants of different areas.

    Analyse the main differences between the ways of speaking of these groups and consider reasons for the differences.

15. Consider the special language associated with a particular job, hobby or sport.

    By giving examples show how the specialist language differs from non-specialist language and say what advantage is gained by the use of specialist language within the group which uses it.

[END OF QUESTION PAPER]

[BLANK PAGE]

[BLANK PAGE]

[BLANK PAGE]

Acknowledgements

Leckie & Leckie is grateful to the copyright holders, as credited, for permission to use their material:
The Sunday Times for the article 'Playing at Guide and Seek' by Sean Newsom, 2001 © NI Syndication, London (2004 Close Reading pp 2–3);
Luath Press for an extract from *The Joy of Hillwalking* by Ralph Storer (2005 Close Reading pp 2–3).

The following companies/individuals have very generously given permission to reproduce their copyright material free of charge:
Brian Millar for the article 'How To Make Science Lovable' (2003 SQP Close Reading pp 2–3);
An extract from *For Love and Money* by Jonathan Raban published by Harvill. Reprinted by permission of The Random House Group Ltd. (2003 Close Reading pp 2–3);
Glenda Cooper for the article 'Women and chocolate: Simply made for each other' (2006 Close Reading pp 2–3).